I0530039

The Master's Teaching

Straight from God's Word.

TIMELESS TRUTH ▪ BOOK 2

Timeless Truth Book 2: The Master's Teaching

Published by Love Worth Finding Ministries, Inc.
2941 Kate Bond Rd
Memphis TN 38133-4017
(800) 274-5683

QUESTIONS

JESUS' PARABLES

A FAITHFUL SERVANT TO THE MASTER TEACHER

The Master's Teaching is an invitation to sit at the feet of the Master, Jesus Christ, guided by the voice of Pastor Adrian Rogers, who devoted his life to helping others know the heart of the Savior.

Few have communicated the depth and relevance of Jesus' teachings more effectively than Pastor Rogers. Known for his warm Southern style, biblical conviction, and Spirit-led wisdom, Pastor Rogers spent decades unveiling the timeless truths of Scripture, making the teachings of Christ accessible and transformational for everyday life.

This book brings together three foundational aspects of Jesus' instruction: the Lord's Prayer, the Beatitudes, and some of His parables.

In the Lord's Prayer, Pastor Rogers saw not a prayer to memorize but a model to follow. For him, it was a masterclass in spiritual priorities—beginning with worship, aligning with God's will, asking for provision, confessing sins, and seeking guidance. He taught that prayer is not about manipulating God, but about fellowshipping with Him, and that through the Holy Spirit, we are empowered to pray according to God's desires. Pastor Rogers emphasized that the Beatitudes, found in Matthew 5, are not about outward achievement but inward character. The Beatitudes represent not a to-do list, but a to-be list, offering a divine portrait of the kind of person God blesses. Pastor Rogers reminded us that spiritual poverty, meekness, mercy, and a hunger for righteousness are signs of a heart rightly related to God, and that true blessedness comes not from worldly success but from a deep, dependent relationship with Christ.

Pastor Rogers described parables as "earthly stories with heavenly meanings." Through familiar images such as seeds, lost coins, and prodigal sons, Jesus revealed profound truths about the human heart and the Kingdom of God. Pastor Rogers explored how Jesus used parables to call us to self-examination, repentance, and faithfulness. He urged believers not to treat these stories as ancient fables, but rather as divine mirrors that reflect both the character of God and the state of our own souls.

Love Worth Finding's Timeless Truth series utilizes a question-and-answer format to share Pastor Rogers' teaching. While this is not an exhaustive approach to the subjects explored, we hope that some of your most important questions will be answered!

The Lord's Prayer

WHY DO WE CALL GOD "FATHER" WHEN WE PRAY?

"Our Father in Heaven..." (Matthew 6:9a).

When Jesus' disciples asked, "Teach us to pray" (Luke 11:1b), He taught them to begin with "Our Father."

Calling God "Father" expresses His nature. Unlike the distant deity of Aristotle or the unknown force of Huxley, Jesus referred to God as "Father" 167 times. But God is not Father to all; He is Father only to those who have been born again through faith in Jesus Christ. God created all people, but He becomes our Father through spiritual rebirth.

As a Father, God has responsibilities toward His children. Jesus taught that if God feeds the birds, how much more will He care for His children? You are not a beggar; you are a child of God. Along with His care comes His correction. In Hebrews 12, we learn that "whom the LORD loves, He chastens." If you are never corrected, you may not truly be His child. God disciplines His children now, but those who are not His will face judgment later.

A good earthly father disciplines his children because he loves them; he wants them to learn what is right and wrong. Likewise, God corrects those He loves.

God is not only our caretaker and corrector; He is also our companion. Just as a good earthly father, despite a busy schedule, is moved when he hears "daddy" from his child, so is God when we call Him "Abba, Father." That intimate Aramaic term reminds us of the relationship He desires. God never gets too busy to listen or to love.

His compassion is boundless. Like the father who left a note to his estranged daughter before dying that said, "I love you, I forgive you, and I know you love me," God's love waits for us, even when we've been distant.

Finally, when we pray "Our Father," we not only express His nature and expect His nurture, but we also exalt His name. "Hallowed be Thy name." The name above all names is Jesus. We must recognize, reverence, and rely on that name. Jesus said, "Ask anything in My name, I will do it" (John 14:14).

Prayer is powerful not because of who we are, but because of the name we pray in. Like a poor man given a check from a wealthy friend, it's not our condition that matters; it's the name signed at the bottom. When we pray, it is in Jesus' name, so the Father may be glorified in the Son.

So, when you say, "Our Father," remember, you express His nature, expect His nurture, and exalt His name. What a glorious way to pray!

"The time will come, if it hasn't already, when having God answer your prayer becomes the most important thing on Earth. Prayer is more than speaking at God; it's a conversation with Him." ADRIAN ROGERS

 RESOURCE: Listen to Pastor Rogers' message, "When We Say Father."

HOW CAN I PRAY FOR GOD'S WILL AND HIS COMING KINGDOM?

"Your kingdom come. Your will be done on earth as it is in heaven" (Matthew 6:10).

To pray for God's will and His Kingdom is to align your heart, mind, and desires with the sovereign rule, gracious character, and glorious future of God. Praying as Jesus taught us for God's Kingdom to come and for His will to be done on Earth as in Heaven not only expresses longing for God's ultimate reign but also invites us into a life surrendered to His authority. Here's how you can meaningfully pray for God's will and His Kingdom in your daily life:

UNDERSTAND WHAT YOU ARE PRAYING FOR. The Kingdom of God is fourfold:

- **God's Government:** His sovereign rule and authority over all creation.
- **God's Grace:** His mercy and kindness, expressed in forgiveness and help for our weaknesses.
- **God's Goodness:** Righteousness, peace, and joy in the Holy Spirit. (See Romans 14:17.)
- **God's Glory:** His final and eternal reign when Christ returns to rule the Earth.

When you pray for His Kingdom, you're asking for these realities to be manifest in your life and in the world, which means to be made clear, obvious, and demonstrable.

ADOPT THE SURRENDER PRINCIPLE. Effective prayer starts with surrender, not commitment. Commitment implies you're in control, choosing what to give. Surrender means placing your entire life under God's control. Begin your prayer by saying: "Lord, not my will, but Yours be done. I surrender all to You."

Be honest. Ask yourself: Have I truly surrendered, or am I only willing to follow if it fits my plans?

APPLY THE SCRIPTURE PRINCIPLE. God's will is not a mystery. It's revealed in His Word. To pray His will, you must know His Word. Spend time reading the Bible daily, meditating on what it says about His character, His promises, and His purposes. Jesus said, "If you abide in Me, and My words abide in you, you will ask whatever you desire, and it shall be done for you" (John 15:7).

Let Scripture guide and shape your prayers so they reflect His heart.

EMBRACE THE SPIRIT PRINCIPLE. Romans 8:26-27 says the Holy Spirit helps us pray when we don't know how. Ask the Spirit to guide you in your prayers. He aligns your desires with the will of the Father.

Prayer is the Holy Spirit finding the desire in the heart of the Father, placing it in your heart, and returning it to Heaven through you. Pray in the Spirit: surrendered, Scripture-soaked, and Spirit-led.

PRAY BOLDLY FOR THE KINGDOM. Come confidently to the throne of grace (See Hebrews 4:16.), not because you're worthy, but because He is gracious. Ask Him to reign in your heart, your home, your church, your community, and the world. Pray for righteousness, peace, and joy to abound. Pray for Christ's return and the full establishment of His glorious reign on Earth.

In summary, follow these steps:

- **Surrender** your will to God.
- **Study** His Word to know His will.
- **Seek** the Spirit's guidance as you pray.
- **Submit** to His sovereign rule in all things.
- **Stand** in hope for His coming Kingdom.

When you pray this way, you're not only asking for God's future reign; you're participating in it now.

"Prayer is not bending God's will to fit our will. Prayer is finding the will of God and getting in on it." **ADRIAN ROGERS**

 **RESOURCE:** Listen to Pastor Roger's message, "The Coming Kingdom of Christ."

WHAT IS OUR DAILY BREAD?

"Give us this day our daily bread" (Matthew 6:11).

"Daily Bread" is symbolic of any need you have: physical, emotional, or spiritual. While it refers to food, its broader meaning encompasses all necessities for daily living. God delights in meeting your needs, but there is a divine order to how you should approach Him in prayer.

The first step in praying for daily bread is to **establish a proper priority**. The Lord's Prayer begins with God's name, Kingdom, and will..."Thy name, Thy kingdom, Thy will"... before shifting to personal needs: "Our bread, our debts, our temptations." This sequence highlights that God's purposes must take precedence over our petitions. You should not approach God as a celestial bellhop to fulfill personal desires but as the Sovereign whose will should guide your life. In Matthew 6:33, Jesus said, "But seek first the kingdom of God and His righteousness, and all these things shall be added to you." Power in prayer depends on putting God's will first. If your request for daily bread is rooted in a desire to serve God and honor Him, your prayer aligns with divine priority.

The second step is to **express a prayerful petition**. Simply put, ask. Many people do not receive because they do not ask. Prayer is the key to Heaven's treasury. James 4:2b says, "You do not have because you do not ask." Jesus taught us to pray, "Give us this day our daily bread," which means asking for "bread sufficient for us." Not our greed but our need. God provides according to His riches in glory, and not always what we want, but what we truly need. You must come humbly, honestly, and confidently, trusting that God hears and answers prayer.

The third component is to **exercise a personal performance**. Prayer is not a license for laziness. The Bible teaches that if a person will not work, neither should he eat. (See 2 Thessalonians 3:10.) Just as birds must leave the nest and scratch for food, believers must act responsibly and work diligently while trusting God for provision. Faith is not proven by doing nothing, but by doing what you can and trusting God to supply the rest. When you pray for bread, you say "amen" by going out and working.

The final step is to **enjoy a present provision**. The prayer says, "Give us this day our daily bread." Not tomorrow's bread, just today's. This teaches contentment and trust. Like the trolley that stays powered by maintaining contact with the overhead line, the believer stays provided for by remaining connected to God. True security isn't in stockpiles or savings, but in a relationship with "a rich baker," your Heavenly Father. You are called to live by faith, not by full tanks or full barns.

The greatest bread is Jesus Himself. He said, "Man shall not live by bread alone" (Matthew 4:4b), and "I am the bread of life" (John 6:35a). Earthly needs matter, but the deepest hunger is spiritual, and only Christ can satisfy it. So, praying for your daily bread means not only asking for your daily needs but also depending on Jesus as the Bread of Life, your true and lasting provision.

"Answered prayer is not for rebels." ADRIAN ROGERS

 RESOURCE: Listen to Pastor Rogers' message, "How to Pray for Our Daily Bread."

HOW DOES FORGIVING OTHERS SET US FREE?

"And forgive us our debts, as we forgive our debtors"
(Matthew 6:12).

Forgiving others sets us free in Christ because it liberates us from the destructive prisons of guilt and bitterness, allowing God's grace to work through us in powerful and transformative ways. Forgiveness is not merely a kind gesture; it is a spiritual act that reflects the heart of the Gospel and leads to emotional, relational, and spiritual freedom.

Two major forces imprison the human soul: guilt and bitterness. Guilt keeps us chained to our past failures, while bitterness binds us to the wrongs others have done to us. But when we accept God's forgiveness for our sins, we are released from guilt. Likewise, when we forgive others, we are freed from bitterness.

Scripture teaches that sin is a debt. We owe a debt to God we cannot pay, and Jesus, through His sacrifice on the cross, paid that debt on our behalf. When we forgive others, we imitate Christ by canceling the debts others owe us, debts of wrongs, betrayals, or hurts. This act of forgiveness, though costly, is grace in action: giving people not what they deserve, but what they need.

Forgiveness is both a command and a condition. Jesus taught us to pray, "Forgive us our debts, as we forgive our debtors." This means we are asking God to treat us in the same way we treat others. If we withhold our forgiveness, we essentially ask God to withhold His. This prayer reveals that an unforgiving spirit not only hinders our relationship with others but also with God.

There are four compelling reasons to forgive:

- **The Grace Factor:** We forgive because we have been forgiven. God extended grace to us, so we must extend it to others.
- **The Guilt Factor:** Unforgiveness blocks God's forgiveness from flowing into our lives.
- **The Grief Factor:** Bitterness causes deep internal harm; it is an acid that destroys its container. Forgiveness sets us free from that harm.
- **The Gain Factor:** When we forgive, we gain our brother or sister, restore relationships, and reflect God's heart to the world.

Forgiveness also comes with costly requirements: we must forgive freely, without extracting our pound of flesh; fully acknowledge the hurt without minimizing it; and finally, choose never to bring it up again. True forgiveness mirrors how God forgives by remembering our sins no more and not holding them against us.

This freedom is not achieved solely through human willpower. As Philippians 2:13 teaches, "It is God who works in you both to will and to do for His good pleasure."

Forgiveness is divine. As we yield to God's Spirit, He enables us to forgive even those who deeply wound us.

In forgiving others, we reflect Christ, break the chains of bitterness, and open the floodgates of God's grace in our lives. The result is release, reconciliation, and revival. Forgiveness isn't just for the offender; it is the path to freedom for the one who forgives.

"In forgiving, you set a prisoner free and then you discover that the prisoner is you." **ADRIAN ROGERS**

 **RESOURCE:** Listen to Pastor Rogers' message, "The Freedom of Forgiveness."

WHAT IS EVIL AND HOW DO I PRAY AGAINST IT?

"And do not lead us into temptation, but deliver us from the evil one" (Matthew 6:13a).

Evil is not merely a vague concept or a symbolic representation of bad things. According to Scripture, evil is personal, powerful, and purposeful. Jesus taught us to pray, "Deliver us from the evil one," clearly identifying evil as an active force rooted in a personal being, Satan.

Evil, then, is organized rebellion against God, orchestrated by Satan and conducted through deception, destruction, and the distortion of truth. Satan is described in the Bible as "the deceiver," "the liar," "the murderer," "the accuser," and "the tempter." He is not merely symbolic but a real, intelligent, and strategic being bent on opposing God and destroying the lives of His people.

The strategy of evil is primarily deception. Satan seeks to blind the minds of people, twist God's truth, and seduce individuals through false doctrines, spiritualism, drugs, compromised media, and complacency. His goal is not just to oppose God but to be worshiped in God's place by setting up counterfeit systems of religion and morality. He operates through "wiles," "devices," and "snares,"—planned attacks tailored to exploit weaknesses.

In response to this reality, Jesus didn't merely offer philosophical answers; He offered a weapon: prayer. When we pray, "Deliver us from evil," we acknowledge our vulnerability and God's sufficiency. Prayer becomes the battleground of spiritual warfare. According to Ephesians 6:12, we do not wrestle against "flesh and blood, but against principalities, against powers, against the rulers of the darkness of this age, against spiritual hosts of wickedness in the heavenly places." Therefore, our primary defense is spiritual: prayer empowered by God's truth.

To pray against evil means to start our day with prayer. We are to ask God to keep us from temptation before we fall into it. Just as we ask for daily bread, we should ask for daily deliverance. Too often, people fall into sin and then ask for forgiveness, repeating the same cycle. Jesus' prayer teaches us to seek prevention, not just a cure.

Effective prayer against evil involves three key components:

- **Recognize the sinister person of evil.** Know your enemy. Satan is real and dangerous, and pretending he doesn't exist only makes you more vulnerable.
- **Realize the seductive power of evil.** Understand that evil doesn't always appear threatening; sometimes it comes through comfort, compromise, or entertainment. It's subtle and often disguised as light.
- **Rely on sovereign protection from God.** The prayer ends with, "For Yours is the kingdom and the power and the glory forever. Amen" (Matthew 6:13b). Victory over evil doesn't rest in our strength but in God's. We rely on His authority and power to shield us and deliver us.

The heart of this prayer is dependence: daily, intentional, humble dependence on God for strength, discernment, and rescue. Evil is real. But so is God's power. When we pray with sincerity and consistency, God promises to deliver us from the evil one. The battle is real, but so is the victory for those who watch and pray.

> "As Christians, we must be in collision with the devil, not in collusion with him." **ADRIAN ROGERS**

 **RESOURCE:** Listen to Pastor Rogers' message, "Victorious Prayer."

WHY DOES THE LORD'S PRAYER END WITH GOD'S KINGDOM, POWER, AND GLORY?

"For Yours is the kingdom and the power and the glory forever. Amen" (Matthew 6:13b).

The Lord's Prayer ends with a triumphant declaration of God's supreme authority, infinite power, and eternal glory. This conclusion is not merely a poetic ending; it's a bold and foundational affirmation of who God is and why we can trust Him completely in prayer.

First, the phrase, **"Yours is the kingdom" reaffirms that God is the sovereign ruler over all.** His authority is absolute and eternal. In a world filled with chaos, temptation, and spiritual opposition, acknowledging God's Kingdom is a way of anchoring ourselves in the truth that no matter how fierce the battle, God reigns. The message is clear: Satan may be active, but he operates in a doomed domain. His rebellion is real, but his defeat is certain because the Kingdom belongs to God. The Lord's Prayer thus closes not with fear, but with confidence in the God who rules over Heaven and Earth.

Second, **"Yours is the power" speaks to God's omnipotence**. While the enemy may appear powerful, Scripture repeatedly emphasizes that God's power is unmatched. Verses like Genesis 18:14a, "Is anything too hard for the LORD?" and Jeremiah 32:17, "Ah, Lord GOD! Behold, You have made the heavens and the earth by Your great power and outstretched arm. There is nothing too hard for You," confirm that nothing is beyond God's ability. God's power is not merely theoretical; it's a dynamic force available to believers. We don't produce power; we release it by aligning with God through prayer. Prayer is the pipeline that connects us with divine strength. That's why Satan's strategy is to keep believers from praying: if we pray, we access God's power, and the enemy is defeated.

Third, **"Thine is the glory" directs our attention to the purpose behind prayer and everything else in the Christian life:** God's glory. John 14:13 says, "Whatsoever ye shall ask in my name, that will I do, that the Father may be glorified in the Son." The key to answered prayer lies in this alignment: when our deepest desire is to see God glorified, and that matches His desire, we can be assured of His response. Prayer, then, becomes not a way to manipulate God for personal desires, but a way to partner with Him in His redemptive work for His glory.

Finally, the closing doxology, **"Forever," underscores the eternal nature of God's Kingdom, power, and glory**. These are not temporary attributes. God is not merely a king now, or mighty for a moment, or glorious in one generation. He is THE King, whose rule, might, and splendor endure forever.

The Lord's Prayer begins with intimacy, "Our Father," and ends with majesty, "Yours is the kingdom, and the power, and the glory." It reminds us that prayer is not only about asking for help but also about recognizing who God is. In times of temptation, fear, or weakness, we pray with assurance because the One to whom we pray reigns with authority, acts with power, and deserves all glory forever.

"Behind any command of God is the omnipotent power of God and the infinite resources of God to carry it out." **ADRIAN ROGERS**

 **RESOURCE:** Get several copies of the booklet, "Victorious Prayer," to share with your small group or those you disciple in the faith.

The Beatitudes

WHO ARE THE POOR IN SPIRIT?

"Blessed are the poor in spirit, for theirs is the kingdom of heaven" (Matthew 5:3).

To be "poor in spirit" is to recognize one's absolute spiritual bankruptcy before God. It is the acknowledgment that, apart from Christ, we have nothing to offer: no moral credit, no righteousness, no personal merit that can earn our way into God's favor. This concept, introduced by Jesus as the first of the Beatitudes in Matthew 5:3, is the foundational attitude for anyone seeking the true spiritual life found in Christ: "Blessed are the poor in spirit, for theirs is the kingdom of heaven."

Being poor in spirit means seeing ourselves as spiritual beggars. Just as a beggar knows he has nothing and must rely on the mercy of others, so too must we approach God with full awareness that we are dependent on His grace. It is not financial poverty that Jesus praises, but a deep humility that admits we cannot save ourselves or live rightly without divine help. This humility is the opposite of pride, which is the root of many sins and rebellions. All other spiritual blessings flow from this foundational recognition of our need for God.

This poorness of spirit is demonstrated throughout Scripture. Isaiah, upon seeing the holiness of God, cried out in brokenness over his unclean lips. (See Isaiah 6:5.) Peter, encountering Jesus' divine power, fell to his knees and declared his unworthiness. (See Luke 5:8.) The Canaanite woman, humbly likening herself to a dog begging for crumbs, was praised by Jesus for her great faith. (See Matthew 15:26-28.) Each of these examples illustrates how spiritual poverty can lead to dependence, humility, and blessings.

In modern life, we are tempted to find our worth in possessions, success, intelligence, or appearance. Society teaches that our value comes from what we achieve or own. But Jesus turns this thinking on its head. He says that the blessed life, the truly joyful, fulfilled, and eternal life, begins when we stop relying on ourselves and start depending entirely on Him.

To be poor in spirit is also to live in brokenness. This isn't weakness or despair, but a clear-sighted view of our sinful nature and our desperate need for redemption. When we stop pretending that we are spiritually "rich" and face the reality of our need, God meets us there. He does not leave spiritual beggars empty; instead, He fills them with His righteousness and gives them the Kingdom of Heaven.

Ultimately, the poor in spirit are those who cast aside pride and self-reliance. They come to Jesus not with their achievements, but with empty hands and open hearts. And in doing so, they receive the greatest treasure of all: eternal life and intimacy with God. The poor in spirit are blessed, not because of their poverty, but because their poverty drives them to the only One who can truly satisfy their souls.

> "Evangelism is one beggar telling another beggar where to find bread." **ADRIAN ROGERS**

 **RESOURCE:** Listen to Pastor Rogers' message, "When Bankruptcy Becomes a Blessing."

WHY DOES GOD ALLOW US TO MOURN?

"Blessed are those who mourn, for they shall be comforted" (Matthew 5:4).

God allows us to mourn not as an act of cruelty or indifference, but as a vital part of His redemptive and transformative plan for our lives. Mourning, particularly in the biblical sense, is not just about sorrow over pain or loss; it is a spiritual posture that acknowledges our sinfulness and our deep need for God's grace. This verse turns the world's logic upside down and reveals a profound spiritual truth: Mourning, when godly, leads to comfort, repentance, and a deeper relationship with God.

At its core, godly mourning is sorrow over sin, our own and the world's. We often try to shield ourselves from pain using distractions like entertainment, achievement, or even self-medication. But the Bible calls us to mourn what grieves God. In doing so, we align our hearts with His and begin to see the world through His eyes. This type of mourning is not self-pity or general sadness, but brokenness over the fact that our sin separates us from God and has real consequences for ourselves and others.

God allows this kind of mourning to refine our character. In a perfect environment like the Garden of Eden, Adam and Eve still fell into sin, proving that ideal circumstances don't produce godliness. Instead, God uses mourning to grow us spiritually. Mourning reveals the truth about our condition and leads us to repentance, which is the path to restoration.

Without mourning, there is no repentance; without repentance, there is no salvation.

Importantly, godly sorrow leads to life. As 2 Corinthians 7:10 explains, "For godly sorrow produces repentance leading to salvation, not to be regretted; but the sorrow of the world produces death." Worldly sorrow focuses on consequences and regrets; godly sorrow turns our hearts toward God. Judas Iscariot regretted betraying Jesus and was consumed by remorse, yet he lacked genuine repentance and ultimately ended in despair. In contrast, Peter wept bitterly after denying Christ but repented and was restored.

God also allows us to mourn so that He can comfort us. His comfort is not mere consolation; it is strength, healing, and empowerment through the Holy Spirit. As Jesus promised in John 14:16-17, the Spirit lives within believers, reminding them of forgiveness, walking beside them, and advocating on their behalf. Mourning invites the Spirit's ministry into our lives, where He brings hope out of sorrow and joy out of repentance.

Mourning draws us into deeper dependence on Christ. It opens our eyes to the reality of sin and the beauty of the cross. When we mourn rightly, God turns our tears into telescopes, helping us see Calvary clearly. In our brokenness, He meets us with grace, comfort, and strength, not to leave us there, but to lift us higher.

God allows us to mourn not to harm us, but to heal us. Through mourning, we are blessed because it brings us to repentance, leads us to Jesus, and opens us to the comfort only God can give.

> "Religion without repentance is repugnant to God." **ADRIAN ROGERS**

 **RESOURCE:** Listen to Pastor Rogers' message, "Turning Tears into Telescopes."

WHAT DOES "MEEK" MEAN?

**"Blessed are the meek, for they shall inherit the earth"
(Matthew 5:5).**

Meekness, often misunderstood as weakness, actually signifies strength under control. "Meekness" means being yielded, surrendering one's strength, ambitions, and desires to God's authority. Jesus exemplified meekness, not through powerlessness, but through power perfectly restrained and directed by divine purpose. He was bold, strong, and courageous, fasting for 40 days, cleansing the temple, and enduring the cross, but He always submitted to God's will. Similarly, Moses, who was considered meek, was a strong leader who faced danger and led an entire nation through the wilderness. Meekness, then, is not about lack of power; it is about mastering power through submission to God.

Meekness is mighty because it channels human strength into divine purpose. Instead of being wild or self-serving, the meek are like trained horses: strong, useful, and responsive to the guidance of the Master. Spiritually, meekness allows us to inherit the richest blessings of life in Christ. This inheritance is not merely material but deeply spiritual: peace, joy, purpose, and eternal reward. Meek people are not easily manipulated by fear or temptation because they already possess everything they need in Christ. They live with a deep assurance and strength that worldly losses or gains cannot shake.

To become meek, one must begin with spiritual humility. Jesus presented the Beatitudes in a purposeful order: first, recognize spiritual poverty ("poor in spirit"), then mourn over sin, and then develop meekness. This path leads to brokenness before God, which opens the heart to yield. Practically, one can cultivate meekness by:

- **Submitting to Christ.** Take His yoke, allow Him to lead, and learn from His example.
- **Receiving the Word with Humility.** We're not to use it for personal advantage, but to obey and be transformed.
- **Being Filled with the Holy Spirit.** Meekness is a fruit of the Spirit; it grows when we rely on His guidance.
- **Letting Go of Material Satisfaction**. We find joy and identity in Christ alone, not in earthly possessions or success.

The promise that the meek "will inherit the Earth" is both a present and future reality. Spiritually, the meek already possess everything they need in Christ. Their inheritance is peace, joy, purpose, and victory over sin and temptation. They live with divine contentment, immune to the devil's threats and enticements. In eternity, this promise finds its complete fulfillment: those who follow Christ will reign with Him when He establishes His Kingdom on Earth. Thus, meekness grants access to the richest treasures of both this life and the next, not through dominance or force, but through surrender to God's perfect will.

"Meekness is strength under control." **ADRIAN ROGERS**

 **RESOURCE:** Listen to Pastor Rogers' message, "The Mighty Meek."

WHAT DOES IT MEAN TO HUNGER AND THIRST FOR RIGHTEOUSNESS?

"Blessed are those who hunger and thirst for righteousness, for they shall be filled" (Matthew 5:6).

To hunger and thirst for righteousness is to passionately desire a right relationship with God above all else. Just as our bodies crave food and water, our souls were designed to crave spiritual fulfillment that only comes from Jesus Christ. This longing isn't a casual interest but a deep, persistent need that drives our thoughts, actions, and priorities. This verse reveals that true satisfaction comes not from worldly pursuits but from a yearning for righteousness, embodied fully in Jesus.

Hungering for righteousness begins with recognizing our spiritual malnourishment. The world encourages us to pursue wealth, status, and comfort, yet these pursuits leave us spiritually starved. Righteousness isn't primarily about moral behavior or religious rituals; it's about Jesus Himself. Scripture teaches that Jesus "became for us wisdom from God—and righteousness..." (1 Corinthians 1:30a). To hunger for righteousness is to hunger for Him, to seek His presence, and to desire to be made right before God through faith in Christ.

This hunger brings blessing because it realigns our priorities with God's will. The blessing is not merely a future promise but a present reality. Those who seek righteousness are promised to be "filled"—satisfied, whole, and complete in Christ. This satisfaction transcends circumstances. When we hunger for Christ, He fills us with peace, joy, and purpose that the world cannot offer. As we seek Him first, His Kingdom and His righteousness, everything else falls into place. (See Matthew 6:33.) Our lives gain direction and depth, and we experience the fullness of God in our daily walk.

To be filled with righteousness means we are no longer relying on our efforts to be "good enough" before God. Instead, we receive the righteousness of Christ by grace through faith. This righteousness changes us from the inside out. It satisfies our deepest spiritual hunger and transforms our character to reflect God's holiness. Being filled also means enjoying a continual relationship with Jesus. He becomes not just our Savior, but the source of our daily strength, comfort, and joy.

The pursuit of righteousness doesn't end once we find Christ. Just as physical hunger returns, our spiritual appetite for Christ deepens as we grow in Him. We continue to seek, to learn, and to abide in His Word. As we do, our lives bear the fruit of righteousness: acts of love, humility, and mercy that reflect the character of Jesus.

In short, to hunger and thirst for righteousness is to crave Jesus above all else. That craving brings the greatest blessing: being filled with His righteousness, joy, and peace. It is the secret to true, lasting satisfaction: a feast of the soul found only in Him.

"Some people are going to go to Hell with a chest full of Sunday school attendance pins who have never received the Lord Jesus Christ. They have religion, but they don't have righteousness. They have culture, but they don't have Christ." ADRIAN ROGERS

RESOURCE: Listen to Pastor Rogers' message about righteousness in Christ, "The Secret of Satisfaction."

WHO ARE THE MERCIFUL? WHAT ABOUT THOSE WHO ARE NOT NATURALLY MERCIFUL?

"Blessed are the merciful, for they shall obtain mercy" (Matthew 5:7).

The merciful are those who reflect the heart of God by putting compassion into action. Mercy is not merely a feeling or a passive sentiment; it is a divine attribute that reveals itself through tangible acts of kindness, forgiveness, and helping others. This blessing is not a reward for emotional softness or moral superiority, but a reflection of a heart that has already been transformed by God's mercy.

Mercy is different from justice and grace. Justice is giving people what they deserve, mercy is withholding what they deserve, and grace is giving them what they don't deserve. God's mercy withholds judgment and punishment from sinners, offering forgiveness instead. When we realize how much mercy God has shown us, it compels us to extend that same mercy to others. Those who have truly received mercy are the ones most capable of giving it.

Being merciful is not always easy or natural. For some, mercy may not come instinctively. The Parable of the Good Samaritan illustrates this. Religious leaders such as the priest and the Levite walked by a suffering man, possibly feeling pity, but doing nothing. They were not merciful. But the Samaritan, moved by compassion, cared for the injured man at personal cost. He showed mercy because his compassion led to action.

This story teaches that mercy is not about status or heritage; it is about choosing to act with love and compassion, regardless of one's natural feelings.

For those who are not naturally merciful, the good news is that **mercy can be learned.** It begins by recognizing the mercy one has already received from God. As one grows in spiritual maturity and begins to understand the depth of God's forgiveness, the ability and desire to be merciful also grow. The Bible teaches that mercy and truth are linked. (See Psalm 85:10.) Understanding the truth of our own sinfulness and the mercy shown to us fosters humility and a desire to extend mercy to others. In other words, those who are not naturally merciful can become merciful by drawing near to God and imitating His character.

Mercy is also a choice. Even if one doesn't feel merciful, choosing to act with compassion can lead to a heart transformation. Those who have suffered and received mercy are often the best equipped to show it. By choosing mercy, especially in challenging moments, one becomes more like Christ, who, despite being despised and rejected, gave everything to offer mercy to humanity.

The merciful are not those who are simply soft-hearted by nature, but those who allow God's mercy to change them and flow through them. And those who are not naturally merciful are invited to receive God's mercy afresh, so they too can extend it, grow in it, and be blessed through it.

"The greatest motivation to be what we ought to be is God's sympathetic compassion no matter how much we fail." **ADRIAN ROGERS**

RESOURCE: Listen to Pastor Rogers' message, "The Magnificence of Mercy."

HOW CAN I BE PURE IN HEART?

**"Blessed are the pure in heart, for they shall see God"
(Matthew 5:8).**

To be pure in heart is to live with undivided devotion to God— to have a heart wholly aligned with Him, free from duplicity, hypocrisy, or self-centered desires. Jesus is revealing both a call to personal transformation and a promise of divine intimacy.

Purity of heart begins with integrity, which means having a single purpose and sincerity in our relationship with God. This doesn't mean moral perfection, but rather wholehearted devotion. The original word used for "pure" implies something unmixed: undivided loyalty and authenticity in our inner being. We are not pure when we try to serve two masters or chase both worldly success and spiritual growth. As Jesus warned, "You cannot serve God and mammon" (Matthew 6:24b). A divided heart will always drift toward compromise and away from the presence of God.

But how can one attain this purity when Scripture tells us the heart is "deceitful above all things, and desperately wicked" (Jeremiah 17:9a)? The answer lies not in self-improvement but in spiritual regeneration. The heart is naturally sinful and cannot be purified through mere effort or moral discipline. One needs a heart transplant: a new heart that only Christ can provide. When you come to Jesus in humility, confessing your sin and trusting in His redemptive work, He gives you a new heart (Ezekiel 36:26) and begins the process of sanctification from within.

King David is a powerful example. Though he committed grievous sins, he remained "a man after God's own heart"

(1 Samuel 13:14a) because of his sincere repentance and single-minded pursuit of God. When confronted with his wrongdoing, David didn't offer excuses; instead, he cried out, "Create in me a clean heart, O God" (Psalm 51:10a). His integrity wasn't about perfection, but about consistent honesty before God.

As God transforms our hearts, we begin to see Him—not with physical eyes, but through spiritual perception. The pure in heart will "see God" in various ways: in Scripture, in His providence, in creation, and ultimately, face to face in eternity. Purity clears the spiritual fog, enabling us to perceive God's hand in our lives and hear His voice more clearly. As Hebrews 11:27 says of Moses, he "endured as seeing Him who is invisible."

Yet even after salvation, our hearts can drift. We become distracted, double-minded, or cold. But God is merciful. Each time we repent and refocus on Christ, He restores our vision and renews our hearts. Thus, to remain pure in heart requires ongoing surrender, honest self-examination, and communion with Christ.

In summary, to be pure in heart is to live with a single focus on God, made possible through salvation in Jesus and cultivated through daily surrender. And the reward of that purity is the greatest of all promises: we will see God.

"Nobody drifts into purity; you have
to choose." ADRIAN ROGERS

 RESOURCE: Listen to Pastor Rogers' message on purity of heart, "Integrity: Don't Leave Home Without It."

HOW CAN I BECOME
A PEACEMAKER?

"Blessed are the peacemakers, for they shall be called sons of God" (Matthew 5:9).

Becoming a peacemaker begins not with external actions but with an internal transformation. According to Scripture, peace is not something we manufacture or achieve on our own; it is something we receive through a right relationship with God. To fulfill this calling, we must first understand peace, its adversaries, and how to share it.

The first step to becoming a peacemaker is to make peace with God. Human conflict, whether with others, within ourselves, or with the world, originates from a deeper spiritual conflict: enmity with God. James 4:1 explains that wars and fights come from our own selfish desires. Until we are reconciled with God through Jesus Christ, we will remain at war in our hearts and contribute to discord in the world.

Peace is not simply the absence of conflict. It is not appeasement or a temporary truce. True peace is a byproduct of righteousness, a heart aligned with God. Hebrews 7 describes Melchizedek, a biblical foreshadowing of Christ, as "king of righteousness" and then "king of peace." This order is essential: peace flows from righteousness. Only those who are pure in heart can truly promote peace. As James 3:18 states, "The fruit of righteousness is sown in peace by those who make peace."

Becoming a peacemaker also means recognizing sin as the adversary of peace. Sin separates us from God and others. It's impossible to have lasting peace while clinging to unrighteousness. Jesus did not come to tolerate sin but to conquer it. He said, "I did not come to bring peace but a sword" (Matthew 10:34b), emphasizing that true peace requires confronting sin, not ignoring it. Just like a conquering army will demand surrender before accepting peace, we must lay down our sin before Christ to receive His peace.

Once we are at peace with God through salvation, we are called to become agents of peace. This is not a passive role; it's an active ministry. As 2 Corinthians 5:18b states, God "has given us the ministry of reconciliation." We are His ambassadors, called to build bridges between people and point them to Jesus. The peace we receive is meant to be shared.

Lastly, peacemaking must be a priority in our lives. As Corrie Ten Boom once said, "If you look at the world, you'll be distressed. If you look within, you'll be depressed. If you look at God, you'll be at rest." Peace starts by looking to God, surrendering our sins, and allowing His Spirit to fill us. Then, and only then, can we bring His peace into a troubled world. To become a peacemaker, begin with Christ, live a life of righteousness, reject sin, and share the peace you've received. Peacemakers aren't born; they are reborn through Christ.

> "Until you are right with God, you will be a troublemaker and not a peacemaker." **ADRIAN ROGERS**

 **RESOURCE:** Listen to Pastor Rogers' message, "The Priority of Peacemaking."

ARE ALL CHRISTIANS PERSECUTED FOR RIGHTEOUSNESS' SAKE?

"Blessed are those who are persecuted for righteousness' sake, for theirs is the kingdom of heaven. Blessed are you when they revile and persecute you, and say all kinds of evil against you falsely for My sake. Rejoice and be exceedingly glad, for great is your reward in heaven, for so they persecuted the prophets who were before you" (Matthew 5:10-12).

Not all Christians are persecuted for righteousness' sake, but all who genuinely live out their faith in Christ should expect some form of persecution. The Bible is clear on this: "All who desire to live godly in Christ Jesus will suffer persecution" (2 Timothy 3:12). This persecution is not a general hardship but suffering that comes specifically because of righteousness, living differently from the world in accordance with Christ's teachings. Some Christians may never face violent persecution or imprisonment, but even in free societies, believers often encounter mockery, marginalization, or loss of opportunities because of their unwavering commitment to godly values.

This means the opposition arises because one is truly reflecting the character of Christ, not because of arrogance, rudeness, or personal wrongdoing. Christians are not blessed for suffering from their own misconduct or for being offensive in the name of faith. True persecution occurs when believers are falsely maligned or specifically mistreated for Jesus' sake, because their godliness and message confront the sinfulness of the world. Jesus warned that if the world persecuted Him, it would also persecute His followers. (See John 15:18-20.)

This kind of persecution, paradoxically, is a blessing. Jesus says, "Blessed are those who are persecuted for righteousness' sake, for theirs is the kingdom of heaven" (Matthew 5:10). This blessing comes in several ways.

First, persecution affirms that a believer is genuinely aligned with Christ. It acts as a spiritual "thermometer," reflecting how closely one walks with God. When Christians stand firm in righteousness and face resistance, they are in the company of the prophets and of Jesus Himself, a mark of deep spiritual authenticity.

Second, persecution brings heavenly reward. Jesus teaches us to "rejoice and be exceedingly glad" because our reward in Heaven will be great. (See Matthew 5:12.) This eternal perspective transforms present suffering into a reason for joy, not despair. It is a mark of honor in God's eyes to be counted worthy to suffer for His name.

Third, how Christians respond to persecution is itself a powerful testimony. Returning love for hate, good for evil, and grace for insult displays the very heart of God. This Spirit-taught response, rather than the natural human impulse to retaliate, can turn persecutors into seekers, as seen in the conversion of Saul (later Paul) after he witnessed Stephen's martyrdom. Persecution refines believers and lends authenticity to their witness, sometimes even softening the hardest hearts.

Persecution for righteousness' sake is a blessing because it proves the genuineness of faith, aligns us with Christ, stores up eternal rewards, and demonstrates God's love to a watching world. Persecution is not to be sought out, but when it comes, it is a cause for joy, not shame.

"Don't get the idea that the world has gotten more churchy if there's no persecution. It's only because the Church has gotten more worldly." **ADRIAN ROGERS**

 **RESOURCE:** Listen to Pastor Rogers' message, "Preparing for Persecution."

Jesus' Parables

WHY DOES JESUS COMPARE PEOPLE TO SHEEP?

"All we like sheep have gone astray; we have turned, every one, to his own way; and the LORD has laid on Him the iniquity of us all" (Isaiah 53:6).

In His teachings and parables, Jesus frequently compared people to sheep and described Himself as the door to the sheepfold, communicating deep spiritual truths in ways that His audience, many of whom were familiar with pastoral life, could easily understand.

Why did Jesus compare people to sheep? In Luke 15, Jesus responds to criticism from the Pharisees for associating with sinners by telling parables that portrayed humanity as sheep. This image wasn't arbitrary. Sheep are known for being defenseless, directionless, and dependent. They need a shepherd for guidance, protection, and rescue. Similarly, Jesus knows people are spiritually lost and vulnerable, in need of divine care and leadership. Isaiah 53:6, "All we like sheep have gone astray..." speaks to the human tendency to wander into sin and self-destruction without divine guidance.

Jesus used the Parable of the Lost Sheep to show the Pharisees why He associated with sinners. Just as a good shepherd leaves the ninety-nine to find one lost animal, Jesus seeks out the spiritually lost. He sees them, lifts them up, and rejoices over their return. In fact, "there will be more joy in heaven over one sinner who repents than over ninety-nine just persons who need no repentance" (Luke 15:7).

This paints a picture of God's passionate concern for every individual and underscores the depth of His grace.

Why did Jesus describe Himself as the door to the sheep? In John 10:7b, Jesus said, "I am the door of the sheep." In biblical times, a shepherd would often lie across the entrance of the sheepfold at night, becoming the literal "door," protecting the sheep from predators and preventing them from wandering off. This imagery symbolizes both access and protection. Jesus as the door means that He is the only legitimate way to enter into salvation, fellowship with God, and eternal life.

This metaphor aligns with Jesus' teaching that He is "the way, the truth, and the life. No one comes to the Father except through Me" (John 14:6). Jesus is not one of many doors; He is the only way to reconciliation with God.

He provides a refuge from sin and death, as described in the concept of cities of refuge in Joshua 20, which also points to Jesus as a safe place for sinners.

Furthermore, the comparison underscores the urgency and compassion in Jesus' mission. In Matthew 9:36, Jesus is "moved with compassion for them, because they were weary and scattered, like sheep having no shepherd." People, without the guidance of Christ, are spiritually aimless and vulnerable.

In conclusion, Jesus compares people to sheep to reveal our need for His guidance and care because of our sinful nature and vulnerability. He describes Himself as the door to the sheep to declare that He alone is the way to spiritual safety, salvation, and a restored relationship with God. These analogies beautifully demonstrate both the love of Christ and our utter dependence on Him for life, direction, and eternal hope.

> "This building is not the Church. It's just a sheep shed." **ADRIAN ROGERS**

 **RESOURCE:** Read the devotional, "God, Our Gentle Shepherd."

WHAT DO THE SHEPHERD, THE WOMAN, AND THE FATHER HAVE IN COMMON?

"Likewise, I say to you, there is joy in the presence of the angels of God over one sinner who repents" (Luke 15:10).

The shepherd with the lost sheep, the woman with the lost coin, and the father with the prodigal son are all central figures in Jesus' parables found in Luke 15. Although their circumstances differ, they share strikingly similar traits that reveal God's heart toward lost sinners. These three characters all demonstrate deep concern for what is lost, diligent effort in seeking, and overwhelming joy in restoration. Through them, Jesus paints a picture of divine love, relentless pursuit, and the joy of redemption.

First, all three show deep concern for what is lost. The shepherd has a hundred sheep, yet when one goes missing, he doesn't dismiss it as expendable. He leaves the ninety-nine to find the one. (See Luke 15:4.) Likewise, the woman, who has ten silver coins, lit a lamp and swept her house diligently to find the single coin she has lost. (See Luke 15:8.) The father, although not able to chase after his younger son who has gone astray, waits expectantly, watching for his return. His actions when the son comes back—running to him, embracing him, and preparing a feast—show that he has never stopped caring. (See Luke 15:20.) In all three stories, the lost item or person is uniquely valued.

Second, they each put effort into seeking or restoring what is lost. The shepherd actively searches for the sheep "until he finds it," a phrase indicating determination and persistence. (See Luke 15:4.) The description of the woman's actions show the thoroughness of her search. (See Luke 15:8.) Though the father does not go out to seek his son physically, his readiness to forgive and reinstate him shows a heart that has been prepared for reconciliation all along. His eagerness demonstrates that restoration was never in question once the son turned back.

Finally, each figure expresses great joy upon finding or recovering what was lost. The shepherd joyfully carries the sheep home and calls others to celebrate with him. (See Luke 15:5-6.) The woman similarly gathers her friends and neighbors to rejoice over finding her coin. (See Luke 15:9.) The father throws a lavish celebration, saying, "this my son was dead and is alive again; he was lost and is found" (Luke 15:24a). Jesus concludes both the sheep and coin parables by saying there is joy in Heaven over one sinner who repents, highlighting that this joy mirrors God's own response to repentance. (See Luke 15:7, 10.)

The shepherd, the woman, and the father all represent God's loving nature. Their actions teach that God cares deeply for each individual, actively seeks the lost, and rejoices when the sinner is found. These parables are not merely stories of lost things; they are revelations of God's heart. Jesus responds to criticism from religious leaders who disapprove of His association with sinners. Through these stories, He clarifies that God does not abandon the lost, but He seeks them with passion and welcomes them home with joy.

"Sometimes I almost wish I were lost so I could get saved all over again." **ADRIAN ROGERS**

 **RESOURCE:** Listen to Pastor Rogers' message, "The Value of a Soul."

IN THE PARABLE OF THE PRODIGAL SON, WHICH BROTHER IS LOST, THE OLDER OR THE YOUNGER?

"And he said to him, 'Son, you are always with me, and all that I have is yours. It was right that we should make merry and be glad, for your brother was dead and is alive again, and was lost and is found'" (Luke 15:31-32).

In the Parable of the Prodigal Son, both the younger and the older brother are lost, though in quite different ways. The parable begins with the younger son demanding his share of the inheritance, an act that symbolizes rejection of his father's authority. He then leaves home and squanders everything through reckless living. His outward rebellion is clear, visible, and destructive. He ends up feeding pigs, a humiliating job for a Jewish man, and longing to eat their food. Finally, recognizing his brokenness, he decides to return home and ask for forgiveness, not expecting to be treated as a son, but simply as a servant. Instead, the father welcomes him with open arms, restores him fully as a son, and celebrates his return.

While the younger son's lostness is obvious, the older son's condition is more subtle. He has stayed home, followed the rules, and worked dutifully for his father. Yet, when his younger brother returns and is celebrated, the older brother becomes angry and refuses to join the celebration. His bitterness and resentment reveals a heart just as estranged from the father as his brother's has been. He complains, "All these years I've been slaving for you and never disobeyed your orders" (Luke 15:29a, NIV). His words exposes his true motivations, not love for his father, but a desire for reward. His obedience has been transactional. He views himself as a servant earning favor, not as a son enjoying a relationship.

Jesus tells this parable in response to the Pharisees and scribes who have criticized Him for welcoming sinners. (See Luke 15:1-2.) The younger son represents the tax collectors and sinners, those who have openly rebelled but were now turning back to God. The older son represents the religious leaders, those who appears righteous but harbors pride and self-righteousness. In this light, Jesus shows that it is possible to be lost while staying "at home." The older son has been physically near the father but is emotionally distant and spiritually blind.

Both sons need the father's grace. The younger son finds it by humbling himself and returning home. The older son needs to recognize his pride and resentment and come into the celebration. The tragedy is that the parable ends with the older son outside, refusing to go in. Jesus leaves the story open-ended, challenging the Pharisees—and all of us—to examine our hearts.

Both the younger and older sons were lost. The younger was lost in rebellion and sin, while the older was consumed by pride and self-righteousness. The difference at the end of the story is that the younger recognizes his need for grace, while the older doesn't see that he needs it. Jesus' message is clear: whether you are "down and out" or "up and out," you are still lost without the Father's grace. The Father's heart longs for both kinds of lost people, not just to return home, but to enjoy full relationship with Him.

> "Pride drives wedges; humility always builds bridges of love." ADRIAN ROGERS

 **RESOURCE:** Listen to the message, "The Ungrateful Brother."

WHO IS THE GOOD SAMARITAN?

"But a certain Samaritan, as he journeyed, came where he was. And when he saw him, he had compassion. So he went to him and bandaged his wounds, pouring on oil and wine; and he set him on his own animal, brought him to an inn, and took care of him." (Luke 10:33-34).

In the Parable of the Good Samaritan (Luke 10:25-37), Jesus tells the story of a man who is beaten, robbed, and left for dead on the side of the road. While a priest and a Levite, both respected religious figures, pass by without helping, a Samaritan, a man from a group despised by the Jews, stops to help the injured man. He treats the man's wounds, takes him to an inn, and pays for his care. At first glance, the Samaritan appears to be a model of compassion and neighborly love. But at a deeper level, the Good Samaritan is a portrait of Jesus Himself.

Jesus is the ultimate Good Samaritan. He is the one who sees humanity beaten, broken, and dying in sin, and He does something about it. Here are seven ways in which Jesus fulfills the role of the Good Samaritan.

He comes to where we are. Just as the Samaritan journeys down the road and goes to the man, Jesus leaves Heaven and comes to Earth to meet us in our brokenness. He doesn't wait for us to go to Him; He comes to us. (See John 1:14.)

He is moved with compassion. The Samaritan has compassion on the wounded man. (See Luke 10:33.) Throughout the Gospels, Jesus is repeatedly described as being "moved with compassion" when He sees people suffering. (See Matthew 9:36.) His compassion leads to action.

He treats our wounds. The Samaritan pours oil and wine on the man's wounds, symbols of healing and cleansing. Jesus heals the wounds of sin and brokenness through His sacrifice and the work of the Holy Spirit. (See Isaiah 53:5.)

He carries us. The Samaritan puts the wounded man on his own animal. In the same way, Jesus bears our burdens and carries us in our weakness. (See Isaiah 46:4; Matthew 11:28.)

He brings us to a place of safety. The Samaritan takes the man to an inn where he can recover. Jesus brings us into the safety and fellowship of His Church, the place where spiritual healing takes place.

He pays the price for our care. The Samaritan gives money to the innkeeper to cover the man's expenses and promises to pay more if needed. (See Luke 10:35.) Jesus pays the full price for our salvation with His blood and continues to intercede and provide for us. (See Romans 5:8; Hebrews 7:25.)

He is despised yet loving. The Samaritan is from a group hated by the Jews, yet he shows love when others don't. Similarly, Jesus is "despised and rejected by men" (Isaiah 53:3), yet He shows greater love than anyone else.

Jesus uses the parable not only to teach about loving our neighbor, but also to point to Himself as the One who loves us perfectly. We are the wounded traveler, helpless, broken, and dying in sin. The Good Samaritan is Jesus, who sees us, has compassion, and gives everything to restore us. The parable is both a call to mercy and a revelation of the merciful Savior.

"A person who has compassion sees people through the eyes of Christ." **ADRIAN ROGERS**

 **RESOURCE:** Listen to Pastor Rogers' message, "How to be a Good Friend."

WHAT DO JESUS' PARABLES ABOUT THE SOWER, THE TARES, THE MUSTARD SEED, AND THE LEAVEN TEACH ABOUT THE KINGDOM OF HEAVEN?

"Blessed are your eyes for they see, and your ears for they hear; for assuredly, I say to you that many prophets and righteous men desired to see what you see, and did not see it, and to hear what you hear, and did not hear it" (Matthew 13:16-17).

Jesus often uses parables to explain spiritual truths about the Kingdom of Heaven. In Matthew 13, He shares a series of parables—the Sower, the Tares, the Mustard Seed, and the Leaven—that reveal the nature, growth, and challenges of the Kingdom. Together, these stories give a rich, layered understanding of how God's Kingdom operates in the world.

The Parable of the Sower. (See Matthew 13:3-9, 18-23.) This parable illustrates how the message of the Kingdom is received by different kinds of hearts. A farmer sows seed, which falls on four types of soil:

Pathway soil: The seed is eaten by birds, symbolizing people who hear the message but do not understand it; Satan snatches it away.

Rocky soil: The seed sprouts quickly but withers under the sun because of shallow roots. This represents people who receive the message with joy but fall away when trouble comes.

Thorny soil: The seed grows but is choked by thorns, symbolizing people distracted by worldly worries and wealth.

Good soil: The seed bears fruit, producing 30, 60, or 100 times what is sown. These are those who hear, understand, and live by the Word.

LESSON: The Kingdom of Heaven begins with the Word being planted in human hearts. Its success depends on how it is received.

The Parable of the Tares Among the Wheat. (See Matthew 13:24-30, 36-43.) In this parable, a man sows good seed, but an enemy sows tares (weeds) among the wheat. Both grow together until the harvest, when the weeds are separated and burned.

- **The field** represents the world.
- **The good seeds** are the children of the Kingdom.
- **The tares (weeds)** are the children of the devil.
- **The harvest** is the end of the age.
- **The reapers** are angels.

LESSON: Evil and righteousness will coexist in the world until the final judgment. The Kingdom grows even in a world filled with evil, and God will deal with the wicked at the right time.

The Parable of the Mustard Seed. (See Matthew 13:31-32.) Jesus compares the Kingdom to a mustard seed, which is very small but grows into a large tree that birds come to nest in. The mustard seed represents the small beginnings of the Kingdom. The tree symbolizes the surprising, expansive growth of God's Kingdom.

LESSON: The Kingdom of Heaven may start small, such as with Jesus and His few disciples, but it will grow into something great and influential.

The Parable of the Leaven. (See Matthew 13:33.) A woman mixes leaven (yeast) into a large amount of flour until it is all leavened. The leaven represents the transforming power of the Kingdom. The flour represents the world or society being influenced.

LESSON: The Kingdom works quietly and invisibly, yet powerfully transforming everything it touches, just like yeast affects the entire batch of dough.

Together, these parables teach us that the Kingdom begins in individual hearts (Sower). It grows in the presence of both good and evil (Tares). It starts small but grows large and has a significant impact (Mustard Seed). It transforms the world from within (Leaven).

Jesus uses these simple images to reveal profound truths: the Kingdom of Heaven is powerful, patient, and ultimately victorious.

> "A parable is an earthly story with a heavenly meaning." **ADRIAN ROGERS**

RESOURCE: Listen to Pastor Rogers' message, "Mysteries of the Kingdom of Heaven."

IN THE PARABLE OF THE RICH FOOL, DOES JESUS TEACH IT IS "FOOLISH" TO MAKE PLANS FOR THE FUTURE?

"But seek first the kingdom of God and His righteousness, and all these things shall be added to you" (Matthew 6:33).

In Luke 12:16-21, Jesus tells the Parable of the Rich Fool—a story of a man whose land produced a plentiful harvest. The man says to himself, "I will pull down my barns and build greater, and there I will store all my grain and my goods." He then declares, "I will say to my soul, 'Soul, you have many goods laid up for many years; take your ease; eat, drink, and be merry.'" But God says to him, "Fool! This night your soul will be required of you; then whose will those things be which you have provided?" Jesus concludes, "So is he who lays up treasure for himself, and is not rich toward God."

The main point of the parable is that it is foolish to live life without regard for God. The rich man is not condemned for being wealthy or even for storing his harvest. He is called a "fool" because he leaves God out of his plans, trusts entirely in his possessions, and ignores the condition of his soul. He assumes he has many years left, but he doesn't realize his life will end that very night. The parable serves as a warning about spiritual short-sightedness and the dangers of living as if this world is all there is.

Is It Foolish to Plan for the Future? No, Jesus does not teach that it's wrong or foolish to plan ahead. Scripture encourages wisdom, stewardship, and preparation. Proverbs 6:6-8 praises the ant for storing up food in the summer. Proverbs 21:5a says, "The plans of the diligent lead surely to plenty." Jesus Himself speaks about counting the cost before building a tower. (See Luke 14:28.) What makes the man in the parable foolish is not his planning, but his failure to acknowledge God and prepare for eternity. He thinks of his grain, but not of his soul.

How Can We Plan for Earth and Heaven? We are called to be responsible stewards of our time, talents, and treasures on Earth, while also living with eternity in view. Here are some ways to balance both:

- **Acknowledge God in all plans:** Proverbs 3:5-6 says to "trust in the LORD with all your heart,...acknowledge Him, and He shall direct your paths." Every plan should begin with prayer and submission to God's will.
- **Be generous:** The rich fool hoards wealth for himself. Jesus calls us to be "rich toward God" by giving to others and investing in His Kingdom. (See Luke 12:21; Matthew 6:19-21.)
- **Live with eternal priorities:** Use your time and resources to serve God and others. Make choices that reflect eternal values, not just temporary gain.
- **Stay spiritually ready:** Recognize that life is uncertain. Keep your heart right with God through faith in Christ and a life of obedience.

In conclusion, Jesus warns against the arrogance of self-sufficiency and the danger of ignoring eternal realities. The wise person plans for both today and eternity, living each day in light of what matters most.

"Our Lord wants us to have three homes: a family home, a church home, and a heavenly home." **ADRIAN ROGERS**

 **RESOURCE:** Listen to Pastor Rogers' message, "Five Minutes After Death."

WHAT CAN WE LEARN FROM THE PARABLE OF THE MARRIAGE FEAST?

"Let us be glad and rejoice and give Him glory, for the marriage of the Lamb has come, and His wife has made herself ready" (Revelation 19:7).

The Parable of the Marriage Feast in Matthew 22:1-14 is one of Jesus' most powerful lessons about the Kingdom of Heaven, God's invitation to salvation, and how we should live in expectation of Christ's return. In the story, a king prepares a wedding feast for his son and sends servants to invite guests. The first group refuses, some even killing the messengers. The king responds with judgment and then invites anyone willing to come, regardless of their good or bad qualities. One guest, however, is thrown out for not wearing the proper wedding garment.

Here's what we learn:

God's invitation is open to all. The original guests represent Israel's religious leaders, who rejects Jesus. The open invitation to "both bad and good" (Matthew 22:10b) shows that salvation is offered to all, regardless of background or status.

Rejecting God's invitation has serious consequences. Those who ignore or attack the king's messengers are judged. This symbolizes God's judgment on those who scorn His grace.

A response is required. It's not enough to be invited. We must accept and respond with genuine faith and repentance.

God offers the invitation, but each person must personally respond.

We must be clothed in righteousness. The man without a wedding garment is cast out. The garment symbolizes righteousness, the covering provided through faith in Jesus. Attending the feast without it shows a lack of true conversion.

Many are called, but few are chosen. This sobering conclusion highlights that while many hear the Gospel, only those who truly surrender to Christ will be saved.

How Can We Be Prepared for the Wedding Feast? Being ready for Jesus' return means more than just belief; it involves active faith and readiness. Here's how we can prepare:

Accept God's invitation. Believe in Jesus Christ for salvation. Without the "wedding garment" of Christ's righteousness, no one can enter the Kingdom of Heaven. (See Matthew 22:11-14.)

Live a holy life. Salvation should produce transformation. While we are saved only by the gift of grace, we are called to "be holy, for I am holy" (1 Peter 1:16). Prepare for the wedding feast by living in obedience and walking in the Spirit.

Remain watchful and alert. Jesus warns us to stay spiritually awake. (See Matthew 24:42.) The return of Christ will come unexpectedly, so we must be vigilant.

What Should We Be Doing While We Wait? Waiting on Jesus is not a passive state; it's an active faith in motion. Here's what we should be doing:

Share the Gospel. Like the servants in the parable, we are to go out and invite others into God's Kingdom. (See Matthew 28:19-20.)

Serve faithfully. Use your time, talents, and resources for God's glory. Be a faithful steward. (See Luke 12:42-44.)

Encourage one another. As we wait, we are called to build each other up in love and truth. (See Hebrews 10:24-25.)

Pray and grow in faith. Stay connected to God through prayer and His Word. (1 Thessalonians 5:17; 2 Peter 3:18.)

In summary, the Parable of the Marriage Feast teaches us about the urgency of salvation, the need for readiness, and the importance of righteous living while we await Christ's return.

"What you give up is nothing compared to what you get. Who wouldn't give up dirt for diamonds? I'm not inviting you to a funeral; I'm inviting you to a feast. I'm not inviting you to death; I'm inviting you to live." ADRIAN ROGERS

RESOURCE: Listen to Pastor Rogers' message, "The Marriage of the Lamb."

Pastor **Adrian Rogers**' unique ability to apply biblical truth to everyday life is yet unparalleled by other modern teachers. **Love Worth Finding** is dedicated to glorifying God by honoring that legacy and expanding his impact.

LWF produces broadcast, print and digital media that reaches around the globe with the profound truth of the Gospel, simply stated. **The mission: to bring people to Christ and mature them in the faith.**

VISIT US ONLINE AT LWF.ORG

Love Worth Finding Ministries with Adrian Rogers
is pleased to be able to bring you this Bible Study. If
you have found it helpful, we suggest you go to our
website, **lwf.org**.

Peruse our "find answers" **Q&A** "about my life, about
my world" and "about God." Sign up for an **email
challenge** that brings encouragement to your inbox.
Engage in a study from our **Biblical Learning Center**.
Or go to the **LWF Store** for print and digital resources
for yourself and those you love.

Through broadcast, print and digital media, our
reach is global. Our mission is to help people find the
greatest Love worth finding, Jesus Christ, and to help
those who already know Jesus grow in the faith.

BOOKS IN THE TIMELESS TRUTH SERIES

**The journey through His Word continues—
watch for more Timeless Truth books ahead.**

For these and other resources, visit

lwf.org/store

or call **(800) 274-5683**

IF THIS BOOK HAS BEEN A HELP TO YOU, WOULD YOU CONSIDER SOMETHING?

This ministry is made possible because of the generous support of people like you who believe in the mission of Love Worth Finding—to bring people to Christ and mature them in the faith.

Your gift today will help others hear the profound truth of the Gospel...simply stated by Pastor Adrian Rogers.

lwf.org/give

800-274-5683